RED-HOT BIKES

BMW

el Gilpin

FRANKLIN WATTS

This edition 2012

First published in 2007 by
Franklin Watts
338 Euston Road
London NW1 3BH

Franklin Watts Australia
Level 17/207 Kent Street
Sydney NSW 2000

Series editor: Adrian Cole
Series design: Big Blu
Art director: Jonathan Hair

A CIP catalogue record for this book is available from the British Library.

ISBN: 978 1 4451 0737 0

Dewey Classification: 629.227'5

Acknowledgements:
The Publisher would like to thank RBP Limited and BMW

All images © BMW (UK) Limited except p5t: Interfoto
Pressebildagentur/Alamy.

Every attempt has been made to clear copyright. Should there be any
inadvertent omission please apply to the publisher for rectification.

Printed in China

Franklin Watts is a division of Hachette Children's Books,
an Hachette UK company.
www.hachette.co.uk

Contents

A world of BMW   4

BMW F 800 S   6–9

BMW K 1200 GT   10–13

BMW K 1200 R   14–17

BMW K 1200 S   18–21

BMW R 1200 GS Adventure   22–25

BMW R 1200 S   26–29

Glossary   30

Further information   31

Index   32

BMW (Bavarian Motor Works) is a German company. It started out in 1916 by making aeroplane engines. However, by the end of the First World War (1914–18), production of these had been stopped, so BMW explored other areas of manufacturing.

Fresh start

In 1923, BMW produced its first motorcycle, the R 32 Twin. This bike had a new type of engine, with two cylinders that were placed end to end. BMW called this the Boxer engine. The company still makes some bikes with Boxer engines today.

⬆ Each BMW motorbike is made up of dozens of different parts. This man is putting together a K 1200 R at a factory in Germany.

Full throttle facts

Company name: BMW
Year of founding: 1916
First bike model: R 32 Twin

Employees: 100,306
Headquarters: Munich, Germany
Chairman: Joachim Milberg

Company HQ

BMW has its worldwide base in Munich, Germany. The company's headquarters are in the spectacular 4-Cylinder Building, which looks like a gigantic 4-cylinder block from a BMW car engine. In Britain, BMW is based in Bracknell, Berkshire. It also has production plants all over the world and employs 106,575 people in total.

⬆ *The 4-Cylinder Building – BMW's headquarters in Munich, Germany.*

⬆ *The moving parts of a BMW motorbike engine are all checked and tested by robots before the engine is attached to the rest of the bike.*

The 21st century

Today, of course, BMW is a world-famous company, known for making cars as well as motorbikes. It currently has 20 different motorbikes in production – six of the very best are featured in detail in this book.

Tech talk

Bavarian – from a region in south-east Germany.

Production plant – a factory where things are made on a production line.

Robot – a machine that is programmed to work on its own.

Number of bikes sold: 100,000+
Number of models: 20 (2007)

Best-selling model: R 1200 GS / Adventure
Number of motorbike manufacturing plants: 1 (Berlin)

BMW F 800 S

The F 800 S was launched in 2006 and is designed to the very high standards that riders have come to expect from BMW. The bike is the perfect combination of speed, control and fun. It is constructed with lightweight components for a high power-to-weight ratio.

Lightweight engine

The 798 cc parallel-twin engine is a lot lighter than many of the engines fitted to other bikes. However, while it might be lightweight, it is certainly not low on power. The 2-cylinder engine generates 85 hp. Many heavier engines with 4-cylinder engines produce the same level of power.

Tech talk

Components – parts of a machine.

hp – horsepower; the measurement of energy generated by an engine.

Parallel-twin – an engine with cylinders positioned side by side.

Power-to-weight ratio – a calculation of power and weight. A high ratio indicates that the bike has a good performance.

⬆ A rider puts the F 800 S through its paces on the open road.

Full throttle facts

Top speed: 200+ kph
Length: 2,082 mm

Power output: 85 hp
Fuel capacity: 16 litres

Silencers

Parallel-twin engines are smaller and lighter than most other engines, but they also make a lot more noise. To solve this problem, BMW has fitted a large silencer to the exhaust pipe of the F 800 S. Silencers work by capturing and muffling most of the sound produced by an engine. Some noise is still produced, but it is greatly reduced.

⬆ The F 800 S is designed to attract new riders with its sporty look.

Kerb weight: 204 kg
Seat height: 820 mm

Engine capacity: 798 cc 2-cylinder
Gearbox: 6-speed

The F 800 S was designed by BMW to be easy to ride. It is aimed at younger, less experienced riders, who are perhaps buying a large motorbike for the first time. There are several things about the bike that make it easier to ride than other, larger bikes. The main factor is its 798 cc engine. It delivers great acceleration without the need to change up through the gears very often. This makes overtaking quicker and safer, because changing gears takes time.

BMW F 800 S

Clutch lever

Brake lever

Throttle

16-litre fuel tank

Gear selector

Foot brake

Indicator lamps

Liquid-cooled, 798 cc, parallel-twin 2-cylinder engine

Tech talk

Acceleration – speeding up.

Clutch – a device used to change gears.

Gears – a system of cogs linking the engine to the chain, belt or shaft that turns the rear wheel.

Reinforced – strengthened.

Aluminium chassis

Large silencer

Fuel tank cap

Reinforced belt

265 mm single-disc brakes

320 mm double-disc brakes

Belt drive

Most motorbikes are driven either by a chain, like a bicycle,
or by a rotating metal shaft drive. But the F 800 S has a belt
drive. The reinforced belt is very strong and has teeth on it that
turn a ribbed disc on the rear wheel. A belt drive makes less
noise than a chain drive, and also weighs less.

HOT SPOT

2 cylinders
positioned
side by side

Parallel-twin engines

Parallel-twin engines have two 'twin' cylinders,
positioned vertically, side by side. This
arrangement saves space: in a V-twin, the
two cylinders make a V shape, and so take
up more room. BMW's parallel-twin engine
was designed especially for the F 800 S and
another BMW bike, the F 800 ST.

BMW K 1200 GT

GT stands for Gran Turismo. GT motorbikes are touring bikes that are also built for speed. The K 1200 GT combines comfort with power and impressive acceleration, making it perfect for long journeys. The most recent version of the GT features the same engine as that of the K 1200 S (see pages 18–21).

⬆ The K 1200 GT is an elegant machine, despite its size, and is well balanced for maximum control.

Full throttle facts

Top speed: 200+ kph
Length: 2,318 mm

Power output: 152 hp
Fuel capacity: 24 litres

Handlebar controls

Riders need to keep their hands on the handlebars at all times, so bike controls have to be within easy reach. The controls on the right handlebar, which has the throttle built into the hand-grip, include a button with a triangle shape on it. This operates the right indicator lamp. The switch above this button cancels the left or right indicator lamps. There are also switches to warm the handlebar grips and the seats.

Tech talk

Gran turismo – Italian for 'great touring'.

Indicators – lights that flash to indicate the direction in which a rider wants to turn.

Throttle – a device that controls the flow of fuel to an engine – the faster the flow, the higher the speed.

⬆ *The K 1200 GT is available with cruise control, which keeps the bike at a constant speed and is perfect for long journeys.*

Kerb weight: 282 kg
Seat height: 820 mm

Engine capacity: 1157 cc 4-cylinder
Gearbox: 6-speed

Powerful machine

The K 1200 GT has a 4-cylinder engine that produces 152 hp – a huge amount of power for a motorbike. This means that even with a pillion passenger, a full fuel tank and fully-loaded panniers, it has no trouble at all accelerating extremely quickly.

BMW K 1200 GT

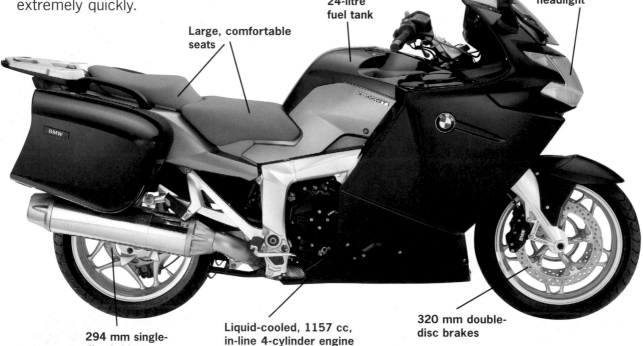

24-litre fuel tank

Large, comfortable seats

Headlight; optional xenon headlight, twice as powerful as a normal headlight

294 mm single-disc brakes

Liquid-cooled, 1157 cc, in-line 4-cylinder engine

320 mm double-disc brakes

HOT SPOT

Clear display

The K 1200 GT has round dial displays showing speed (on the left) and rpm (on the right). Between those is a flat screen display (switched off in this picture). It shows the distance the bike has travelled, called a tripometer, and the fuel level, as well as other information. This bike also has an optional colour-screen satellite navigation system fitted between the handlebars.

Fully adjustable

The K 1200 GT is made for long journeys and so is very comfortable. Seat height, handlebar height and even the windshield height are all adjustable, so a rider can move everything to fit his or her height exactly.

Optional ESA (Electronic Suspension Adjustment), which allows the suspension to be changed to suit the rider

Mirrors

Optional cruise control

Detachable panniers

4-way adjustable handlebars

ABS

The K 1200 GT is fitted with ABS (anti-lock braking system). This is a type of braking system that stops the wheels from locking completely if the brakes are applied suddenly. It is very important for safety. If the wheels were to lock, the bike would skid, throwing the rider and passenger off.

Tech talk

Panniers – storage cases or boxes made to fit on the sides of a bike.

Pillion – the back seat on a motorbike for its passenger.

Rpm – short for revolutions per minute; a measurement of the speed of a motorbike's engine.

Satellite navigation – an electronic system that uses satellites to show exactly where the bike is travelling.

Xenon – a type of gas that creates bright, white light.

BMW K 1200 R

The K 1200 R is all about raw power. In fact, with its huge 4-cylinder engine offering 163 hp, it is the most powerful production roadster built by any motorbike company. The K 1200 R's design is stripped down, or 'naked', and it is this that gives the bike its aggressive styling.

⬆ *The K 1200 R is a powerful roadster.*

Full throttle facts

Top speed: 200+ kph
Length: 2,228 mm

Power output: 163 hp
Fuel capacity: 19 litres

↑ The K 1200 R has been cleverly designed to give a tough appearance with minimum weight.

Lateral thinking

The 1157 cc engine in the K 1200 R is fitted across the frame, with an extreme lean angle of 55 degrees (from upright). This means the weight of the engine is carried low on the chassis, making the bike well balanced. The extra space between the front wheel and the engine has allowed BMW designers to add a large airbox, which assists in maintaining the correct engine temperature.

HOT SPOT

Aluminium chassis

The K 1200 R might look like a tough heavyweight, but its aluminium chassis is lightweight. That doesn't mean that it is weak, though. Aluminium is a very strong metal and can easily support the other parts of the bike that are attached to it. The K 1200 R has its engine – the heaviest part of the bike – carried low on the chassis. This gives the bike a well-balanced ride that is easier to control.

Tech talk

Airbox – a device used to direct air onto the engine.

Roadster – a large, stripped-down bike, also called a 'naked' bike because it has few fairings.

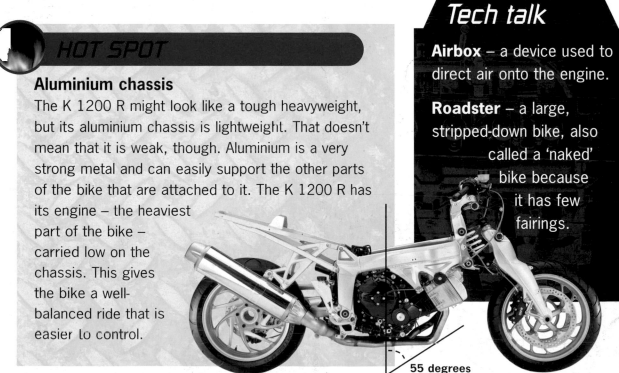

55 degrees

Kerb weight: 237 kg
Seat height: 820 mm

Engine capacity: 1157 cc 4-cylinder
Gearbox: 6-speed

Unique styling

The K 1200 R is a hugely powerful muscle bike, unlike anything BMW has built before. Its styling is very different from the other motorbikes the company makes. In many other ways, however, the K 1200 R is not so different. It has the same engine as the K 1200 S superbike, for example, and shares many other parts with different bikes from the BMW range. The K 1200 R comes in three colours: dark graphite, sun yellow (shown) and white aluminium.

BMW K 1200 R

Eye-catching twin headlights

Airbox

Centre stand (in the down position)

Flat seat for pillion passenger

6-speed gearbox

Front fork wind covers

265 mm single-disc brakes

Liquid-cooled, 1157 cc, in-line 4-cylinder engine

10-spoke aluminium wheels

320 mm double-disc brakes

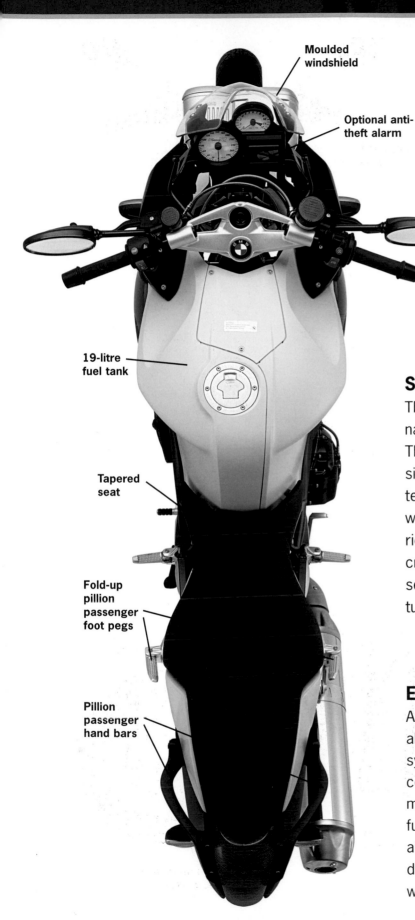

Moulded
windshield

Optional anti-
theft alarm

19-litre
fuel tank

Tapered
seat

Fold-up
pillion
passenger
foot pegs

Pillion
passenger
hand bars

Seat shape

The K1200 R has a seat that is tapered – narrow at the front and wider at the back. There is a good reason for this. When sitting up and driving more slowly, a rider tends to slide to the back of the seat. It is wider here to give more comfort. When a rider is going fast, however, he or she crouches down at the front. Because the seat is narrower here, it allows riders to tuck in their legs, reducing wind resistance.

Exhaust system

Although the K 1200 R is powerful, it is also environmentally friendly. The exhaust system, for example, has a catalytic converter built in (as do all BMW motorbikes). This treats the exhaust fumes before they are released into the air and converts (changes) the most dangerous gases into safer ones. In this way, it helps to reduce pollution.

BMW K 1200 S

The K 1200 S has set new records for BMW. In November 2005, a test rider drove one across the Bonneville Salt Flats in New Jersey, USA, at 283 kph. This is the fastest speed ever achieved by any production BMW motorbike.

The K 1200 S is BMW's fastest production motorbike, and has enough power to carry a passenger comfortably.

Full throttle facts

Top speed: 200+ kph
Length: 2,282 mm

Power output: 167 hp
Fuel capacity: 19 litres

Fairings

Most sports motorbikes have fairings. The fairing is the structure that wraps around the front and sides of a bike, containing the headlight and windshield. It makes the bike more streamlined, pushing the air past the rider's legs and body. It also offers the rider's legs some protection if the bike topples over.

⬆ *The K 1200 S harnesses the power of its 1157 cc engine, producing quick acceleration.*

Fast and safe

The K 1200 S is a sports machine built for the road. It is extremely fast and has incredible acceleration (0–97 kph in just 2.8 seconds). The K 1200 S is more comfortable and safer than most other bikes of its size, which are built for the racing track and then sold as road machines. Among other safety features, it has ABS as an optional extra.

Tech talk

Production motorbike – a motorbike built in large numbers for sale to the general public.

Kerb weight: 248 kg
Seat height: 820 mm

Engine capacity: 1157 cc 4-cylinder
Gearbox: 6-speed

BMW K 1200 S

Optional Electronic Suspension Adjustment (ESA)

Duolever front suspension system (see below)

Liquid-cooled 1157 cc, in-line 4-cylinder engine (hidden under fairing)

Duolever front suspension

The K 1200 S features a special BMW front suspension system called Duolever. It separates the wheel control and suspension functions. This improves rider control by reducing the amount the front suspension dips when the rider brakes heavily. It also makes the steering more controllable.

ESA

The K 1200 S can be fitted with an Electronic Suspension Adjustment (ESA) system. It has nine settings, which can be easily changed while on the move. These are designed for different types of riding and load. They vary from sport, through normal and comfort, to special settings for use when carrying a passenger and luggage.

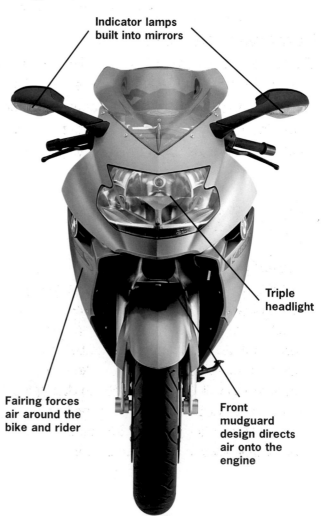

Indicator lamps built into mirrors

Triple headlight

Fairing forces air around the bike and rider

Front mudguard design directs air onto the engine

The BMW Paralever brace sits above the swing arm, which conceals the shaft drive

Paralever rear suspension

The K 1200 S features BMW's Paralever rear suspension. As with the front system, it improves handling, but the Paralever does this by making adjustments according to the load weight. It also powers the rear wheel by a shaft drive concealed inside the swing arm.

Shaft drive

Many BMW motorbikes feature a shaft drive. This is a solid, metal rod that runs from the engine to power the rear wheel, instead of a chain or belt.

HOT SPOT

Headlights

Headlights enable riders to see where they are going at night, but they also have another important function – telling car drivers that bikes are coming up behind them. In many countries, motorbike riders must travel with bike headlights on during the day. The K 1200 S has three headlights built into one unit, one set comes on automatically when the bike is started.

The R 1200 GS Adventure is an endurance tourer, built for long journeys over rough terrain. It is designed to survive even the roughest treatment. Its chassis is made from cast aluminium and tubular steel for strength, and it has special protective guards around the engine. Although it looks like a specialist bike it is a very popular model. This is partly because it is not only exciting and looks great, but is also very comfortable to ride on the road.

Solid history

BMW launched its first endurance machine – the R 80 G/S – in 1980. It went on to win the Dakar rally several times before being updated with the first R 1200 GS model in 2004. The newest R 1200 GS Adventure has a huge travelling range. In theory it could travel over 700 kilometres on one tank of fuel.

⬆ The R 1200 GS Adventure has no trouble on dirt tracks. This bike is fitted with optional sidelights.

Full throttle facts

Top speed: 200+ kph
Length: 2,210 mm

Power output: 100 hp
Fuel capacity: 33 litres

Tough panniers

The panniers and top boxes of most bikes are designed for streamlining and good looks. Those of the R 1200 GS Adventure are built from aluminium for strength. On off-road journeys, a rider may skid and topple over. The boxes that carry their kit have to be strong enough to withstand this rough treatment.

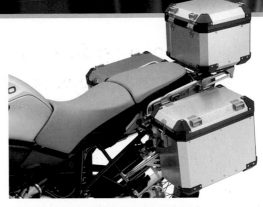

Tech talk

Dakar rally – a world-famous endurance race.

Endurance – to cope with rough treatment, such as riding off-road.

⬆ The R 1200 GS Adventure rides well on and off the road. Here you can see its knobbly tyres.

Kerb weight: 256 kg
Seat height: 895 mm

Engine capacity: 1170 cc 2-cylinder
Gearbox: 6-speed

Riding off-road

The R 1200 GS Adventure has a powerful engine and high ground clearance, both important for a bike meant to be ridden off-road. It also has tough, knobbly tyres to give grip even on slippery ground. The front of the R 1200 GS Adventure has a double mudguard, with a traditional mudguard close to the top of the wheel and a second mudshield sticking out from the front of the bike. The rear wheel also has an extra mini-mudguard to reduce the amount of spray that comes off it.

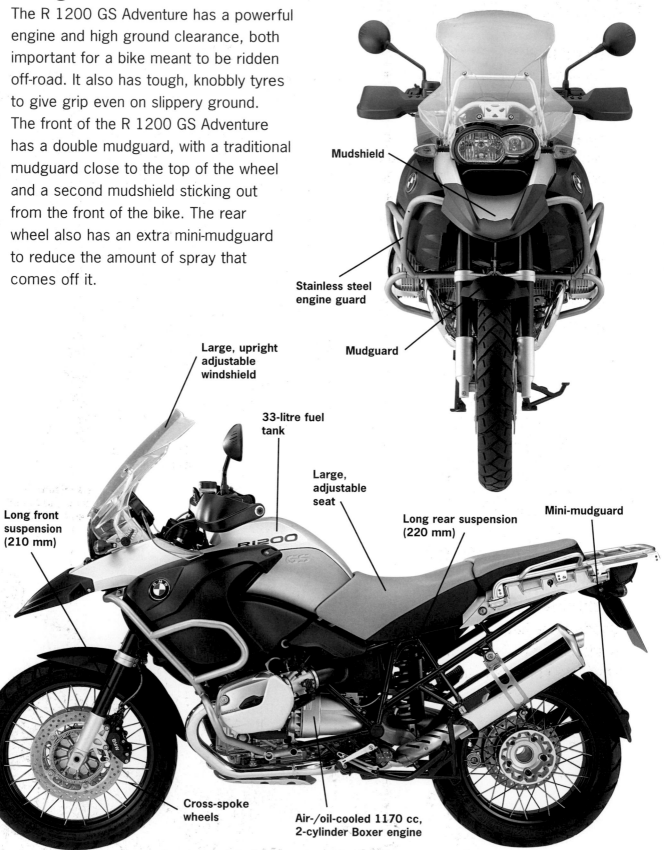

Mudshield

Stainless steel engine guard

Mudguard

Large, upright adjustable windshield

33-litre fuel tank

Large, adjustable seat

Long front suspension (210 mm)

Long rear suspension (220 mm)

Mini-mudguard

Cross-spoke wheels

Air-/oil-cooled 1170 cc, 2-cylinder Boxer engine

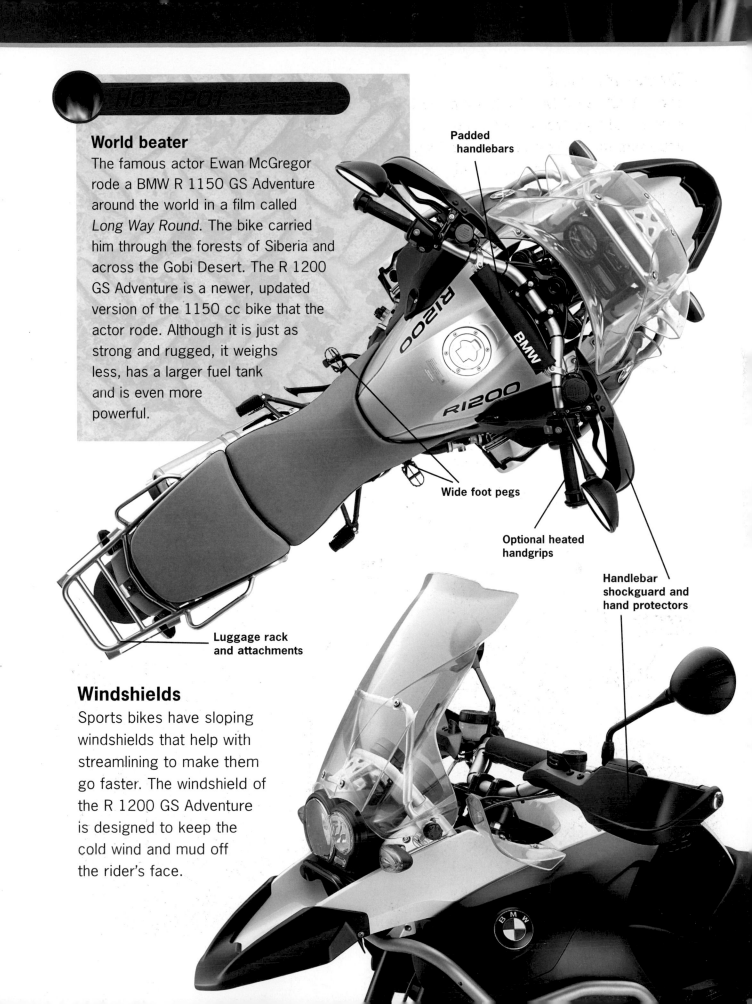

World beater

The famous actor Ewan McGregor rode a BMW R 1150 GS Adventure around the world in a film called *Long Way Round*. The bike carried him through the forests of Siberia and across the Gobi Desert. The R 1200 GS Adventure is a newer, updated version of the 1150 cc bike that the actor rode. Although it is just as strong and rugged, it weighs less, has a larger fuel tank and is even more powerful.

Padded handlebars

Wide foot pegs

Optional heated handgrips

Handlebar shockguard and hand protectors

Luggage rack and attachments

Windshields

Sports bikes have sloping windshields that help with streamlining to make them go faster. The windshield of the R 1200 GS Adventure is designed to keep the cold wind and mud off the rider's face.

BMW R 1200 S

One look at the R 1200 S tells you that it is a sports machine. Lightweight and streamlined, with a bucket seat that invites the rider to lean forward, it is built for speed and acceleration. The R 1200 S is more at home on the track than perhaps any other bike that BMW makes. Its 1170 cc, 2-cylinder Boxer engine generates 122 hp at a maximum 8,800 revs per minute. The bike is perfectly balanced for riding through tight corners, tilting over to a 52-degree riding angle.

⬆ *The kidney-shaped front grille of the R 1200 S is also seen on BMW cars.*

Full throttle facts

Top speed: 200+ kph
Length: 2,151 mm

Power output: 122 hp
Fuel capacity: 17 litres

Crash helmets

The crash helmet is one of a motorbike owner's most important possessions. Riders hope they will never need it, but if they do it could save their lives. Crash helmets come in a huge range of colours and many different designs. Some have chin guards, while others do not. Most crash helmets have a flip-down visor, which keeps the wind, rain and debris out of the rider's face.

Tech talk

Bucket seat – a seat that holds a rider or driver in place.

Chin guard – the part of a crash helmet that goes around in front of the chin.

Visor – a see-through screen on a crash helmet.

Although made for one, this bike can carry a passenger. Note the extra foot pegs – the left one can be seen folded back in this photo, just behind the rider's boot.

Kerb weight: 213 kg
Seat height: 83 mm

Engine capacity: 1170 cc 2-cylinder
Gearbox: 6-speed

Racing style

The R 1200 S is designed mainly for a single rider – everything about it is intended for a crouched-over, streamlined riding position. The hand grips on the handlebars, for instance, are low, and the fuel tank is moulded to perfectly fit a rider's crouching body. The narrow chassis also helps with streamlining by allowing the legs to be held in tight against the bike. The seat has been designed to give the rider greater control into turns, and narrows to allow him or her to easily touch the ground when at a stop.

R 1200 S

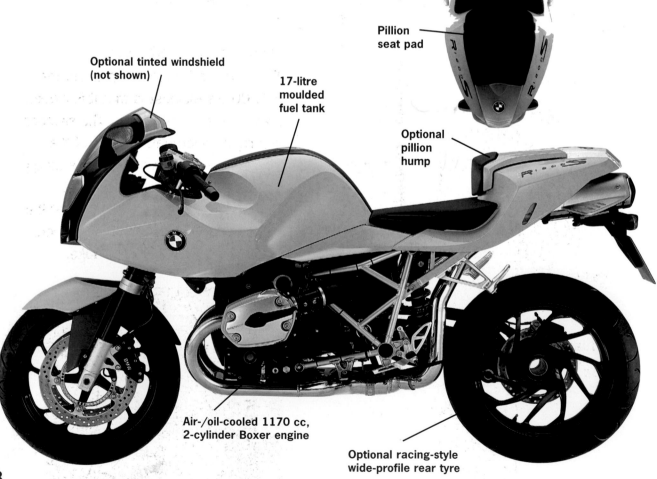

Cylinders of the Boxer engine

Pillion seat pad

Optional tinted windshield (not shown)

17-litre moulded fuel tank

Optional pillion hump

Air-/oil-cooled 1170 cc, 2-cylinder Boxer engine

Optional racing-style wide-profile rear tyre

R 1200 S white dials

The speedometer (left-hand dial) and the tachometer (right-hand dial) of the R 1200 S have been given a sporty look. The red needle and white background relay information quickly to the rider. There is even an electronic screen that displays the distance travelled, fuel level and oil temperature. The panel above the display shows the current gear (this bike is in neutral).

18-LED rear light that shines red when the lights are on or the brake is applied

Exhaust mounted under the tail

BMW R 1200 S

Optional ABS that can be turned off when not required

Underslung exhaust

The most noticeable thing about the R 1200 S's exhaust is that it is hidden away, like on a race bike. The silencer sits right underneath the tail of the bike, rather than out to the side as on most other models. The exhaust system takes away the fumes that the engine produces. Without it, the rider would be surrounded by smoke.

Tech talk

LED – short for Light Emitting Diode. It produces a small amount of very bright, coloured light.

Neutral – the position when a gear has not been selected.

Glossary

Anti-lock braking system (ABS) – an electronic system that prevents a vehicle's wheels locking and improves control when braking hard.

As standard – a manufacturer uses this phrase to refer to the equipment that comes with a bike straight from the factory. Also see entry for 'optional'.

Catalytic converter – also called a 'cat', this device removes most poisonous gases from an engine's exhaust fumes, before they are released into the air.

cc – short for cubic centimetres, it is used as a measurement of the size of the engine's cylinders.

Chassis – the basic frame or structure of a motorbike to which all other components are attached.

Cruise control – an electronic system that fixes the speed of a bike, especially useful on long, open roads.

Cylinders – the places in an engine where fuel and air are ignited to generate power.

ESA – Electronic Suspension Adjustment – BMW's suspension control system that changes to make the ride smoother or firmer, even when the bike is travelling.

Fairing – a shell, usually made of plastic, fitted over the frame of some motorbikes to direct the air around the bike and rider.

Horsepower (hp) – the measurement of energy generated by an engine.

Optional – in this sense, when a particular feature is available at an extra cost. Also see entry for 'as standard'.

Pillion – the back seat on a motorbike for its passenger.

Speedometer – displays the speed at which the bike is travelling, usually in kilometres per hour (kph).

Suspension – the system of springs, shock absorbers and other components, directly connected to the wheels or the axles to help create a smooth ride.

Swing arm – a movable strut between the frame of the motorbike and the rear wheel assembly.

Tachometer – displays the speed of the engine in revolutions per minute (rpm).

Tripometer – displays the distance travelled, which can be reset to zero by the rider.

Websites

http://www.bmbikes.co.uk/
A huge website full of information on BMW motorbikes.

http://www.bmw-motorrad.co.uk/gb/en/index.html
The official website of BMW motorbikes in the UK. Includes a 'virtual centre' where you can build your own fantasy BMW bike.

http://www.worldofbmw.com
BMW's website. Motorbike news, travel stories and information on BMW's riding skills courses.

http://www.bmwmotorcycles.com
The official website of BMW motorbikes in the USA. It has detailed information and pictures of all the motorbikes in the company's current range.

http://www.thebmwclub.org.uk
The website of the BMW Club (UK and Ireland), featuring historical BMW motorbike photographs.

Books

BMW Motorcycles: The Evolution of Excellence
Kevin Ash (Whitehorse Press, 2006).
The complete story of BMW and its involvement with motorbike manufacture and development.

BMW Racing
Mick Walker (The Crowood Press, 2003).
A great account of BMW's finest years on the racing circuits of the world.

The BMW Story
Ian Falloon (Haynes Group, 2003).
A detailed look at the history of BMW racing and production motorcycles, from 1923 to the present day.

BMW timeline

1916 – BMW is formed under the name Bayerische Flugzeug-Werke (BFW). The company builds aeroplane engines.

1917 – BFW is renamed BMW (Bavarian Motor Works) and adopts the logo it still has today, representing an aeroplane propeller in the blue sky.

1923 – BMW launches its first motorbike, the R 32.

1924 – BMW wins its first German motorbike racing championship.

1935 – For the first time, the company produces more than 10,000 bikes in a single year.

1937 – Ernst Henne sets a new motorbike land speed record of 278 kph riding a modified BMW. His record stood for 14 years.

1938 – BMW delivers its 100,000th motorbike from the production line.

1945 – BMW stops producing motorbikes following the Second World War (1939–45).

1948 – Motorbike manufacture officially begins again at BMW with the launch of the R 24.

1960 – The R 69 S is launched. It is still considered by many to be the 'classic' BMW motorbike.

1969 – Motorbike production moves to a new factory in Spandau, Berlin. BMW first offers colour options on its bikes.

1976 – The 1000 cc, R 100 RS is launched, the world's first production motorbike with a full fairing.

1981 – A BMW off-road motorbike, the R 80 G/S, wins its first Dakar rally.

1991 – BMW produces its 1,000,000th motorbike.

1997 – The R 1200 C is launched and features in the James Bond film *Tomorrow Never Dies*.

2004 – The K 1200 S and R 1200 GS are launched.

2005 – The K 1200 R is launched.

2006 – The F 800 S, K 1200 GT, R 1200 GS Adventure and R 1200 S are launched.

2007 – The G 650 series, K 1200 Sport and HP2 Megamoto are launched.

2011 – New models K1600GT and K1600GTL are introduced – the first motorcycles powered by a 6-cylinder engine.

Index

acceleration 8, 10, 12, 19, 26

anti-lock braking system (ABS) 13, 19, 29, 30

anti-theft alarm 17

belt drive 9

brakes 8, 9, 12, 16, 20, 29

catalytic converter 17, 30

chassis 9, 15, 22, 28, 30

clutch 8

crash helmets 27

cruise control 11, 13

cylinders 4, 6, 7, 8, 9, 12, 14, 15, 16, 19, 20, 23, 24, 26, 28, 30

Dakar rally 22, 23, 31

Electronic Suspension Adjustment (ESA) 13, 20, 30

endurance 22, 23

engine 4, 5, 6, 8, 10, 12, 15, 16, 19, 20, 21, 22, 24, 29

Boxer engine 4, 24, 26, 28

capacity 7, 11, 14, 15, 19, 23

noise 7, 9

parallel-twin 6, 7, 8, 9

temperature 15

exhaust 7, 17, 29

fairings 15, 19, 20, 30, 31

foot pegs 17, 25, 27

fuel capacity 6, 10, 14, 18, 22, 26

fuel tank 8, 9, 12, 17, 22, 24, 25, 28

gearbox 7, 11, 15, 16, 19, 23, 27

gears 8, 29

ground clearance 6, 10, 14, 18, 22, 24, 26

handlebars 11, 12, 13, 25, 28

warming 11, 25

hazard warning lights 11

headlights 12, 16, 19, 20, 21

horsepower (hp) 6, 12, 14, 26, 30

indicator lamps 8, 11, 20

motorbikes

F 800 S 6–9, 31

F 800 ST 9

K 1200 GT 10–13, 31

K 1200 R 4, 14–17, 31

K 1200 S 10, 16, 18–21, 31

R 1150 GS Adventure 25

R 1200 GS Adventure 5, 22–25, 31

R 1200 S 26–29, 31

R 32 Twin 4, 31

R 80 G/S 22, 31

mudguard 20, 24

naked motorbikes 14, 15

panniers 12, 13, 23

pillion 12, 13, 16, 17, 28, 30

power-to-weight ratio 6

production motorbikes 14, 18, 19, 31

racing 19, 23, 31

rpm 12, 26

satellite navigation 12, 13

seat 7, 11, 12, 13, 15, 17, 19, 23, 24, 26, 27, 28

shaft drive 9, 21

sidelights 22

silencer 7, 9, 29

skidding 13, 23

speed 6, 10, 11, 12, 14, 17, 18, 22, 25, 26, 31

speedometer 29, 30

streamlining 19, 23, 25, 26, 28

suspension 13, 20, 21, 24, 30

swing arm 21, 30

tachometer 29, 30

throttle 8, 11, 30

tripometer 12, 30

tyres 24, 28

wheels 8, 9, 13, 15, 16, 20, 21, 24

windshield 13, 17, 19, 24, 25, 28